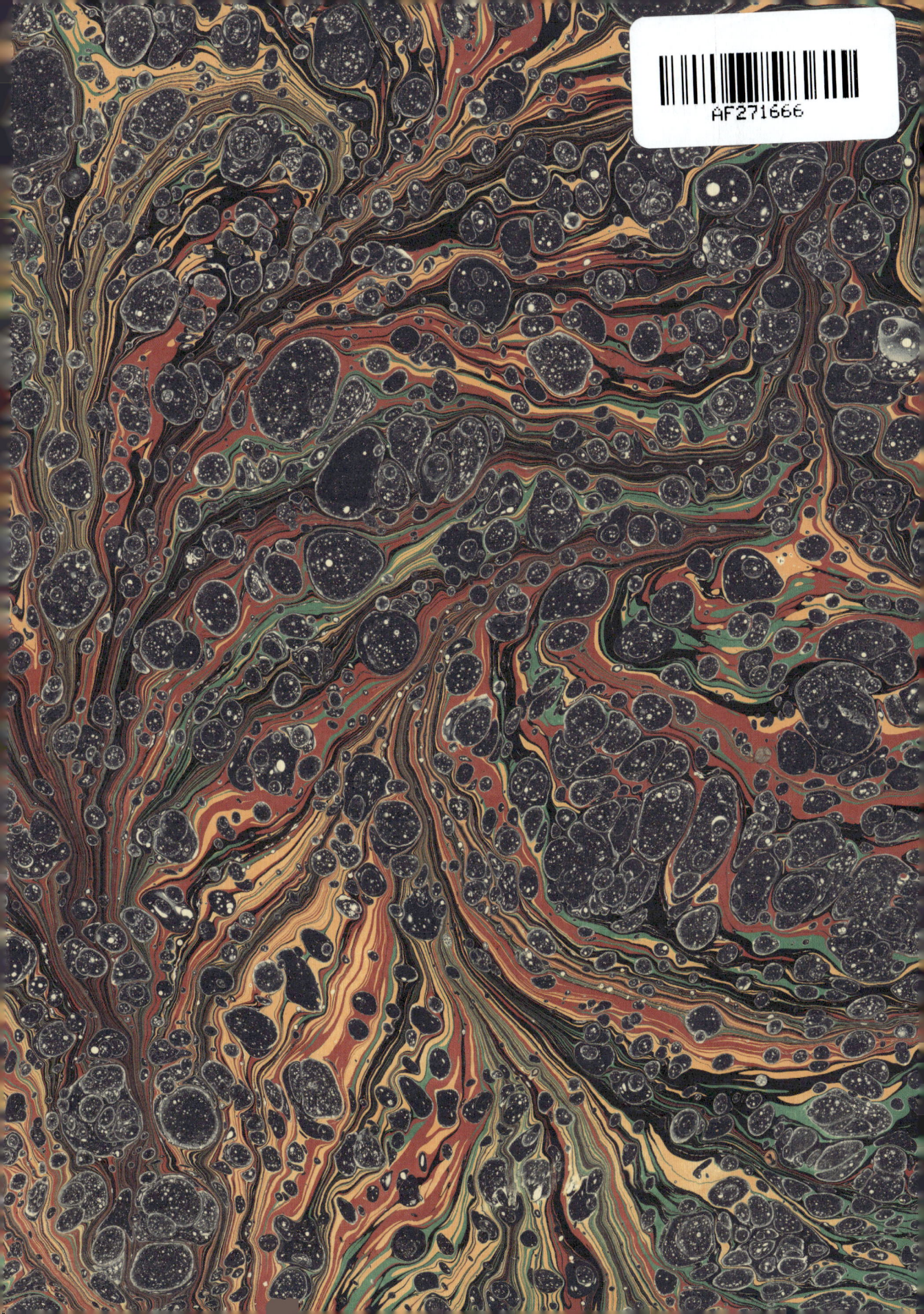

ASSAULT BADGES
OF THE GERMAN ARMY
IN WORLD WAR II

Rolf Michaelis

Schiffer Military History
Atglen, PA

Translation from the German by Dr. Edward Force.

Book Design by Stephanie Daugherty.

Copyright © 2012 by Schiffer Publishing.
Library of Congress Control Number: 2012942404

Printed in China.
ISBN: 978-0-7643-4257-8

This book was originally published in German under the title
Die Sturmabzeichen des Heeres by Michaelis-Verlag.

We are interested in hearing from authors with book ideas on related topics.

Published by Schiffer Publishing Ltd.
4880 Lower Valley Road
Atglen, PA 19310
Phone: (610) 593-1777
FAX: (610) 593-2002
E-mail: Info@schifferbooks.com.
Visit our web site at: www.schifferbooks.com
Please write for a free catalog.
This book may be purchased from the publisher.
Try your bookstore first.

In Europe, Schiffer books are distributed by:
Bushwood Books
6 Marksbury Avenue
Kew Gardens
Surrey TW9 4JF, England
Phone: 44 (0) 20 8392-8585
FAX: 44 (0) 20 8392-9876
E-mail: Info@bushwoodbooks.co.uk.
Visit our website at: www.bushwoodbooks.co.uk

CONTENTS

FOREWORD

During the Polish campaign, which lasted only six weeks, the Supreme Commander of the Army intended to create new military badges that were to honor individual brave deeds and services of the soldiers more specifically. Thus, for example, the Infantry Assault and Panzer Assault Badges were introduced on December 20, 1939. After the campaign against France various versions – bronze and silver – plus a new badge: the Assault Badge (general) came to be awarded. As the war went on, higher levels of the Panzer and Assault (general) Badges were given.

Earning the Assault Badge placed high demands on the soldiers. The psychological and physical burdens that went with an assault attack are scarcely associated with the badge any more today.

One should remember that the probability of being killed or wounded in an assault was considerably higher than to fight off an assault in a well-built position. This meant that only a few Assault Badge awards for twenty-five and more days of action could be made.

Rolf Michaelis
Berlin, January 1998

HISTORY OF THE ASSAULT BADGE

During World War I the Iron Cross was given for a variety of actions: bravery in assault was honored with this decoration just as steadfastness in defense was. In World War II the soldier's deeds were to be made more clearly recognizable by the introduction of new decorations. The Assault Badge could thus be given to members of:

- the Army

- Waffen-SS and Police units subordinated to the Army

- Eastern peoples as volunteers.

Thus foreigners who served with the Army, Waffen-SS or Police could also be honored, such as:

- Walloons (Belgians) in Infantry Battalion 373

- Finns in the Finnish Volunteer Battalion of the Waffen-SS.

The regimental commanders determined by order for which units a day of action was counted as an assault day. Then the company and battery leaders named those soldiers who had taken part in the attack and entered their names in special lists. When the requirements for qualifying were fulfilled, the lists were turned in to the appropriate superior officers with the nomination for awarding the badge.

While the Infantry Assault Badge were awarded since its origin by regimental commanders (naming the recipients in the regimental orders), the Panzer Assault Badges and Assault Badges (general) were originally to be awarded by division commanders (identifying the recipients in daily division orders). As of September 9, 1942 these Assault Badges could be given by the commanders of individual battalions and regiments. Awards to Eastern people were an exception. Here the badge was awarded by the Commander of the Army.

In every case, certificates of possession were to be issued. Only these gave the right to wear the badges. The day of awarding was to be entered in the man's personal papers, particularly the *soldbuch*. If a man left the unit to go to a hospital because of wounding or illness, or was transferred to another unit, an excerpt from the list was to be added to the transfer papers. The lists were to be continued after the awarding, to make sure of how many assault days the individual soldier had.

Decisive for the awarding of the badges was the fighting action of the soldier in an assault. A strict standard was to be established to be appropriate for the requirements for earning the badge. The basis of it has to be expressible in words. It was stipulated that it was better:

> "through the standard rejection of all applications whose details did not seem to be explained without exception, to deny individual soldiers earned recognition than to lower the value of the badge as recognition for brave service through lax handling."

Duplicate processes or replacement of lost badges by purchase could be handled only by presenting the possession certificate, for written applications only by submitting an authorized copy of the possession certificate bearing a service stamp. Unauthorized wearing was punishable according to Paragraph 132 a StGB. Miniature decorations of, for example, 16mm size could be worn on civilian clothing.

When the qualifying requirements had been met, the soldier was to be awarded the Assault Badge as quickly as possible. In case of wounds, the badge along with the document was sent to the hospital for awarding. If the address of the hospital was unknown to the field troop unit, the badge with the document was to be sent to the replacement troop unit after four weeks. Some of them, though, were sent directly to the soldier's home address.

If a missing soldier could no longer be awarded the badge, then after six weeks it was to be sent to the family. While it was arranged that only the OKH was responsible for the awarding of military medals to prisoners of war or interned members of the Army, this rule did not apply to the Assault Badge. Here the appropriate superior officer could take charge of the badge. The badge and document were then sent to the next of kin.

The Assault Badge could also be awarded posthumously if the soldier had fulfilled the required conditions. They were also regarded as fulfilled if he had died on the third assault. The documents and badges were likewise to be sent to the next of kin.

The longer the war lasted, the more specific the requirements for qualification became. After soldiers had moved to other service arms by command or transfer, the question arose as to whether the Assault Badge to be awarded there should be qualified for again or not. On May 12, 1941 the OKH thereby stated that a soldier could earn only one of the various assault badges. The awarding of one Assault Badge thus ruled out the awarding of the other. If a soldier was credited with two assault days in a tank-destroyer unit and then transferred to the tank-destroyer unit of an infantry regiment, he did not receive the general Assault Badge, but rather the one that applied to the service arm to which he belonged in his last action. Here it was the Infantry Assault Badge in Silver. But if a soldier was only temporarily ordered to a different service arm, he received the Assault Badge applying to his own service arm; for example, if a member of the assault guns was ordered to a tank unit. In this case he was to receive the general Assault Badge and not the Panzer Assault Badge in Silver.

With the attack on the Soviet Union, fighting against tanks took on a special significance. To encourage this, the OKH ordered on October 23, 1941 that personal action in the destruction of enemy tanks in close combat with close-combat weapons qualified as an assault attack in the sense of the qualifications for awarding the Assault Badge. This ruling, though, was no longer valid with the introduction of the special badge for destroying enemy tanks on March 9, 1942.

Also linked with the attack on the Soviet Union was the confrontation of the German soldier with a new means of waging war: partisan fighting, which grew to a large extent chiefly in eastern and southeastern Europe and confronted the German command with very difficult tasks. The basic principle was that partisan fighting fulfilled the conditions for earning the Assault Badge as long as the enemy possessed heavy weapons – in regard to the Panzer Assault Badge, particularly anti-tank weapons. On January 30, 1944 partisan fighting was removed from the conditions for awarding the Assault Badge, as on that day Hitler established the Anti-Partisan Badge as a decoration for bravery and achievement.

THE INFANTRY ASSAULT BADGE

On December 20, 1939 the commander of the Army, *Generaloberst* von Brauchitsch, ordered the introduction of the Infantry Assault Badge:

> "as a visible sign of recognition of the infantryman who proved himself in assault attack, but at the same time as an impetus to the highest fulfillment of duty."

The Infantry Assault Badge could, according to the awarding regulations of December 20, 1939, be awarded to officers, non-commissioned officers and men of the rifle companies of non-motorized infantry divisions and the mountain rifle companies, who as of January 1, 1940 had taken part:

– in three assault attacks

– in the foremost line

– with weapon in hand, breaking in

– on three different combat days

Successful power investigations plus counterthrusts and counterattacks were to be counted as assault attacks as long as they had resulted in close combat. A short time later the awardings were also extended to infantrymen and grenadiers of independent battalions, etc., which were not directly subordinated to any division.

An Infantry Assault Badge showed a rifle with fixed bayonet, surrounded by an oval oak-leaf wreath, on the upper part of which the emblem of the Wehrmacht was located. It was worn on the left side of the chest and at first was made of non-ferrous metal. During the war fine zinc came to be used to manufacture it. In addition, so-called half-full or hollow-pressed badges were also made. The reason for this development was chiefly the material shortage that was making itself noticeable in the German war economy.

On June 1, 1940 the awarding of the Infantry Assault Badge was modified. For one thing, the badge could now also be awarded to members of the heavy (machine-gun, infantry-gun or antitank-gun) companies of the infantry and mountain hunter regiments – here as the Infantry Assault Badge in Silver; for another, also to members of the motorized infantry and mountain rifle regiments – under the same conditions they received the Infantry Assault Badge in Bronze.

As a rule, the men of the heavy weapons, who prepared the breakthrough with their heavy weapons, but did not take part in the assault itself, did not meet the requirements for earning the Infantry Assault Badge, *"with weapon in hand, breaking in"* and *"in the foremost line"*. In special cases, though, these soldiers could also be awarded the Infantry Assault Badge if they, sent into close combat with their weapons, fought under the same combat conditions as the penetrating grenadiers.

INFANTRY ASSAULT BADGE

Silver   to members of the non-motorized infantry, grenadier or mountain rifle regiments

Bronze   to members of the motorized infantry, armored grenadier or mountain rifle regiments

---

The former *SS-Junker* Günter Adam remembers:

> "On June 22, 1941 I was a member of an infantry gun company. Belonging to the 1st Platoon, we were assigned to an advance group. The 2nd Platoon to the 1st Battalion, the 2nd Platoon to the 2nd Battalion, and the 4th Platoon to the 3rd Battalion. The 13th (IG) Companies, like the 14th (*Panzerjäger*) and 16th (Engineer) Companies, were never used complete, but always assigned to support. The advance unit, though, was always the 15th (Motorcycle) Company. Through these subordination conditions, subordinated units were always the stepchildren. Very welcome, but slightly disadvantaged. It was the same when badges were given.

> The Assault Badge existed since 1940. At that time it was not yet required to have a sheet for close combat and assault days glued into the service book. We young soldiers had no idea in any case of the handling of such procedures, and the rushed advance with high losses for us never left us time for such thoughts. Although we looked on somewhat enviously when we saw our comrades of the mountain rifles with their

Left: Prototype of a non-introduced model of the Assault Badge.

Right: Accepted version of the Infantry Assault Badge.

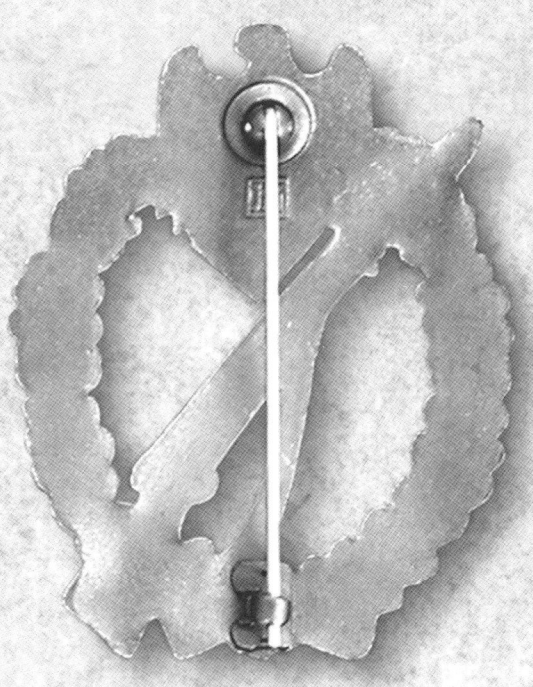

Infantry Assault Badge in Silver (massive version).

Infantry Assault Badge in bronze (hollow-cast version).

Backs of the Infantry Assault Badge in hollow and massive form, with different pin systems.

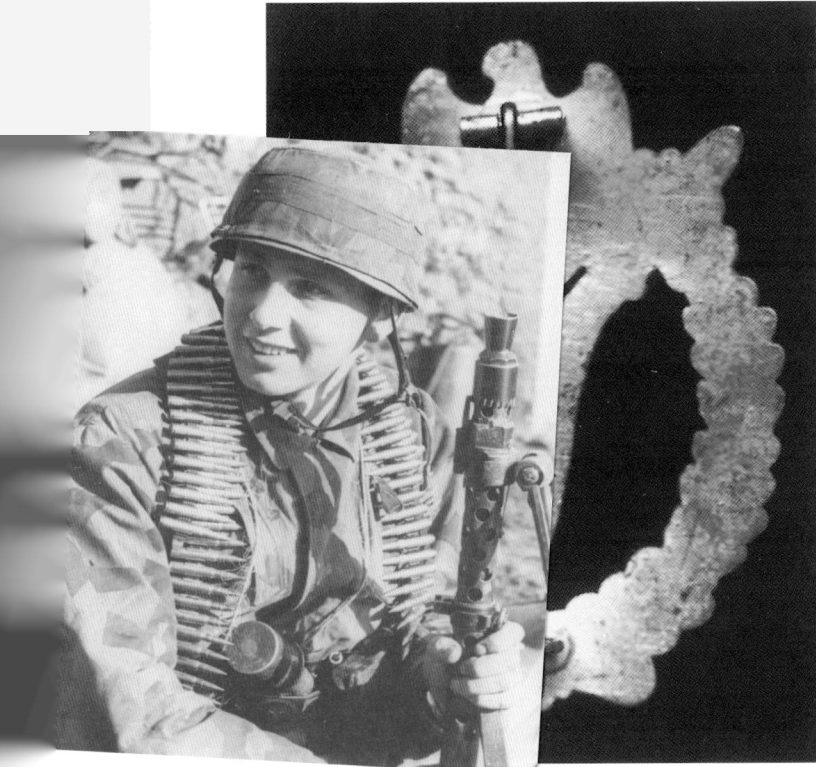

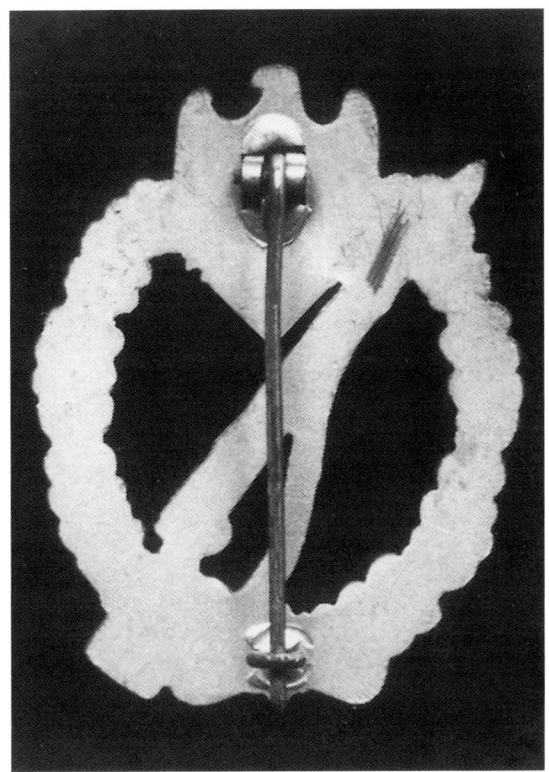

...acks of massive badges with different pin systems.

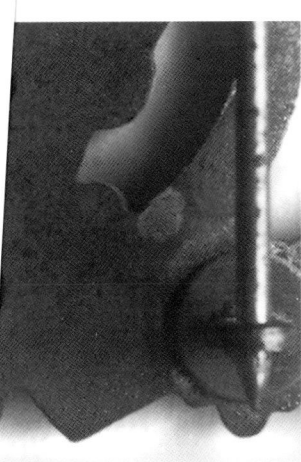

...rk on the gun butt.

13

Georg Kachel – here with the Iron Cross II, the Wound Badge in Black,
and the Infantry Assault Badge in Bronze – received the Close Combat Badge
in Gold on November 15, 1943.

Auf Grund seiner Teilnahme an

drei Sturmangriffen

in vorderster Linie verleihe ich dem

Oberfeldwebel Wolfgang Strößenreuther,

11. / Jnfanterie-Regiment 74

das

Jnfanterie= Sturmabzeichen

Jm Felde, am 24.10.1940.

Schmidt

Oberst und Regiments-Kommandeur

C. Gundlach Aktiengesellschaft, Bielefeld

A special type of award certificate for the Infantry Assault Badge.
Note that there is still no mention on it of the "bronze" or "silver" version.

Dienststelle   Jm Felde, den 5. Januar 1944
der Feldpostnummer 09865 B.

Betr.: Verleihung des Jnf. Sturmabzeichen in Silber.

Herrn
Karl Gebhardt,
Annarode b.Mansfeld,
Kohlenstrasse 110

                        Sehr geehrter Herr Gebhardt !

Jhrem Sohn und unserem lieben Kameraden, Gefr. Heinz Gebhardt, wurde
am 14. 12. 1944, das beiliegende

                        Jnf. Sturmabzeichen in Silber.

verliehen.

Da der Kompanie zur Zeit die neue Lazarettanschrift nicht bekannt ist,
übersendet die Kompanie Jhnen die Auszeichnung mit der Bitte, diese an
die Jhnen bekannte Anschrift weiterzuleiten.

                                        H e i l H i t l e r !

                                        Leutnant u. Kp. – Fhr.

Anlagen:
1 Jnf. Sturmabzeichen in Silber,
1 Urkunde.
Einschreiben!

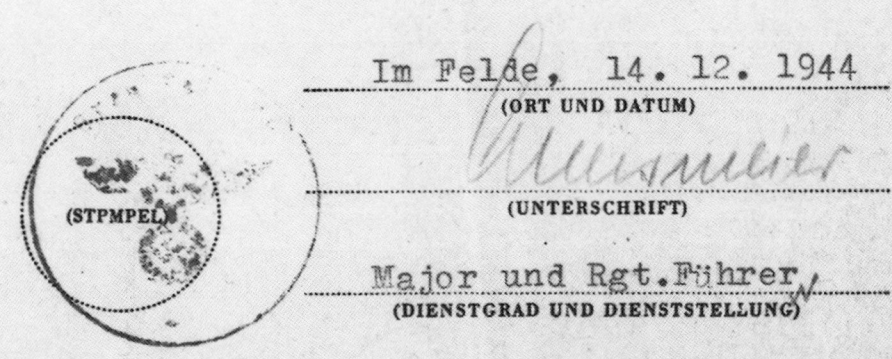

BESITZZEUGNIS

DEM .... Gefreiten ....
(DIENSTGRAD)

Heinz Gebhardt
(VOR- UND ZUNAME)

5. / Grenadier - Regiment 189
(TRUPPENTEIL)

VERLEIHE ICH DAS

INFANTERIE-STURMABZEICHEN

IN SILBER

Im Felde, 14. 12. 1944
(ORT UND DATUM)

(STPMPEL)

(UNTERSCHRIFT)

Major und Rgt. Führer
(DIENSTGRAD UND DIENSTSTELLUNG)

Since the location of the awarded wounded soldiers was unknown, the badges and documents were sent to their fathers to retain.

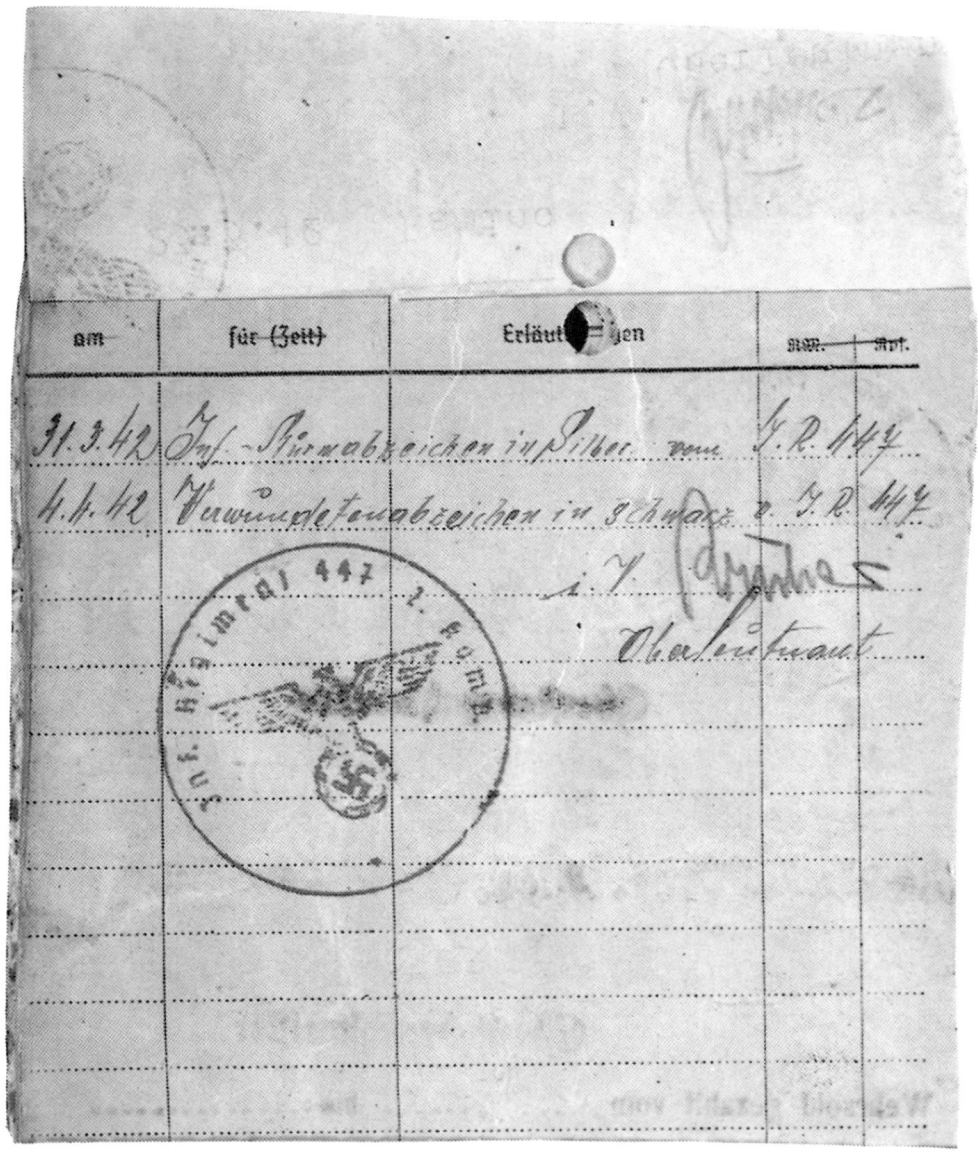

am	für (Zeit)	Erläuterungen	Tag.	Rpf.
31.3.42	Inf.-Sturmabzeichen in Silber	vom J.R. 447		
4.4.42	Verwundetenabzeichen in Schwarz	v. J.R. 447		
		i.V. Oberleutnant		

Soldbuch entry on the awarding of the Infantry Assault Badge in Silver.

silver Infantry Assault Badges, for they did not wear camouflage jackets as we did. Until I was wounded on December 1, 1941, no member of our company had received an Assault Badge. But the assault days that were credited to the individual had to be recorded somewhere. Just without our knowledge. At Christmas 1942 – I was just on recovery leave – the Infantry Assault Badge was sent to me with the award date of September 9, 1942. And this although I had not returned to the old unit after being wounded. Curiously, the award certificate spoke of the "Infantry Assault Badge" without saying whether it was silver or bronze. I got myself a silver one and wore it unchallenged to the war's end – actually, we as a motorized troop were only supposed to wear the bronze badge."

THE PANZER ASSAULT BADGE

On the same day on which the Infantry Assault Badge was introduced, the Commander of the Army approved the introduction of the Panzer Assault Badge. This already had two forerunners: On July 13, 1921 the *Reichswehr* Minister had created the Panzer Badge for, *"remembrance of the achievements of the tank units for the former crews of the German tanks."* As a rule, it was awarded on application to the commanders, the guncrews, the drivers and assemblers and the intelligence personnel of the tanks, as long as three missions were documented. For special achievements, wounding or imprisonment it could also be awarded for fewer than three missions. The badge shows a German A7V tank over which a death's head and crossbones are placed, with a wreath of oak leaves at the left and a laurel wreath to the right. The badge was made partly of silver, brass or copper in massive or hollow form and worn on the left side of the chest.

Just a short time after the Spanish Civil War began on July 18, 1936, a Panzer Corps Badge was introduced for members of tank crews and anti-tank units in the Legion Condor. The commander of the German Panzer troops in Spain (Oberst von Thoma) awarded the badge to the soldiers who had been in the theater of war at least twelve weeks and whose conduct had been unobjectionable at all times. Similarly to the Panzer Badge of 1921, the Panzer Corps Badge of the Legion Condor shows a death's head with crossbones above a tank, surrounded by a wreath of oak leaves. Unlike the previously awarded badge, the background was stamped out and the badge was hollow-pressed. Finished in silver or silver-plated, the Panzer Corps

Badge was also worn on the left side of the chest. It is interesting that the commander of the Army approved it only retroactively on July 10, 1939, *"in recognition of the outstanding achievements of the panzer troops in Spain 1936-39."*

The World War II badge, originally called the Panzerkampfwagen Badge, could be awarded to officers, NCOs and men of the tank units, defined as of January 1, 1940 as:

- Tank or armored command car commanders

- Tank gunners

- Tank drivers

- Tank radiomen

who had proved themselves, actively involved in combat, on three different days.

Holding the Panzer Badge of World War I or the Panzer Corps Badge of the Legion Condor did not depart from the requirements set for the new Panzer Badge.

The Panzer Badge consisted of an oval oak-leaf wreath in which a tank was shown. On the upper part of the wreath was the Army eagle. This badge, like nearly all German decorations, was worn on the left side of the chest. The materials and means of production were identical to those of the Infantry Assault Badge. There were massive pieces of non-ferrous metal and fine zinc, as well as so-called half-full types (made only of fine zinc), plus hollow-pressed badges of sheet metal.

On June 1, 1940 the awarding of the decoration, now called the *Panzerkampfabzeichen*, was extended by a second version. The former specifications now resulted in awarding the Panzer Badge in Silver. A Panzer Badge in Bronze could be awarded as of June 1, 1940 to members of:

- Rifle regiments

- Motorcycle rifle battalions

- Armored scout car units (of the panzer divisions.)

The qualifications for awarding the bronze badge differed from those of the silver version in that the soldiers not only had to have proved themselves in combat three times, but also:

– in three assault attacks

– in the foremost line

– breaking in with weapon in hand

– on three different combat days.

These requirements also were expanded during the war. Members of independent units who belonged to no division were also included among the men who could be honored.

The former *SS-Rottenführer* Eberhard Baumgart (3./SS-Auflk.Abt. "LAH") took part in seventeen assaults. He recalls:

> "One day in the summer of 1943 our division, the "Leibstandarte Adolf Hitler", again prepared for an attack. More and more units moved forward over the runway and fanned out on the terrain. Tanks had already driven up and formed a flat arc. We of the 3./AA, the SPW Company, spread out behind them. The two amphibious companies (1. and 2./AA) moved out to the left and right. Our heavy company lined up in back. I looked around – something great was in the air – but what was right ahead of us, what was going on tactically, what intention from "up above" was being followed by the division's formation, I had absolutely no idea. This lack of an idea about the "cutting and thrusting" that was just ahead of us was generally regretted, not only by me but by all my comrades, all the more so when, in talks wit prisoners – we also met ethnic Germans in the Red Army – it was learned that their Kommissar as a rule made the purpose and goal clear before every attack. I saw how the division set out with motors rumbling, how the regiments moved up and got ready for an assault. I sat in back over the entrance hatch on the frame, let my legs hang down and looked all around. Our *Unterscharführer* stood beside the machine-gun shield and had binoculars to his eyes.

The Panzer Badge of 1921.

An *Oberfeldwebel* wears, among others, the Panzer Troop Badge of the Legion Condor and the Panzer Assault Badge in Silver.

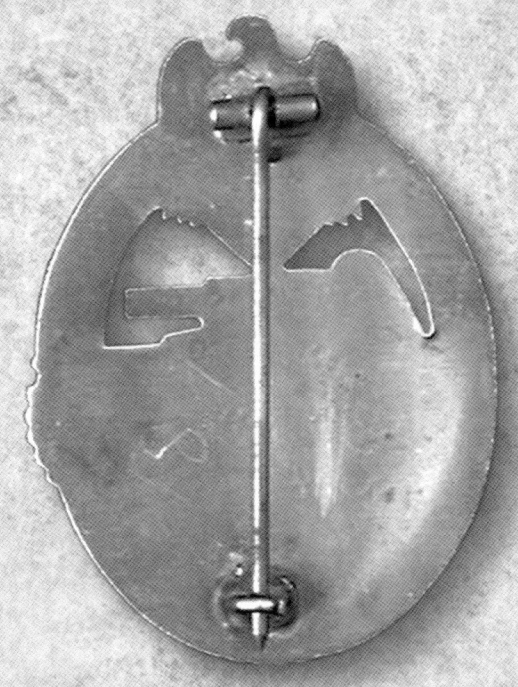

Panzer Assault Badge in Silver (massive version).

Panzer Assault Badge in Bronze (hollow-pressed version).

**Panzer Assault Badge in Silver,
2nd level, for 25 combat days.**

**Panzer Assault Badge in Bronze,
3rd level, for 50 combat days.**

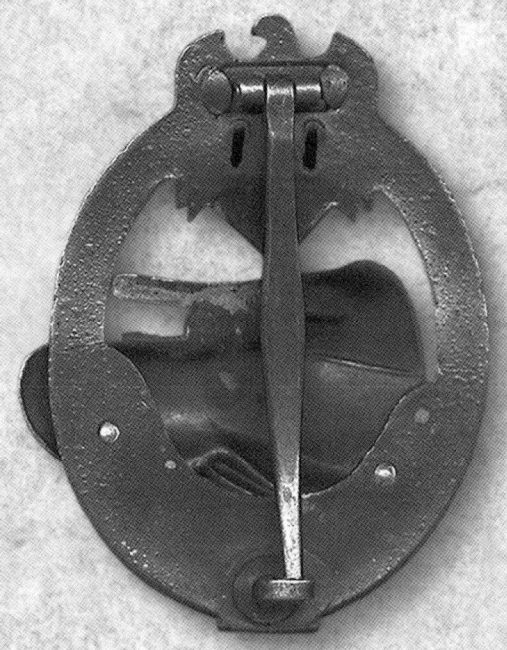

The back of the 2nd and 3rd levels.

**Panzer Assault Badge in Silver,
4th level, for 75 combat days.**

**Panzer Assault Badge in Bronze,
4th level, for 100 combat days.**

The back of the two 4th level badges.

Eberhard Baumgart

Oberstleutnant Hassel wears both the Knight's Cross and, among others, the Panzer Assault Badge in Silver, 3rd level.

A bearer of the Panzer Assault Badge in Silver with number of actions

Besitzzeugnis

Dem .... Oberleutnant ....
(Dienstgrad)

Willi Bröcker
(Vor- und Zuname)

Stab II./Schtz.-Rg. t14o
(Truppenteil)

wurde das

Panzerkampfabzeichen

— Bronze —

verliehen.

Div.Gef.St., den 8.Juli 1942
(Ort und Datum)

(Unterschrift)

Generalmajor u.Div.-Kdr.
(Dienstgrad und Dienststellung)

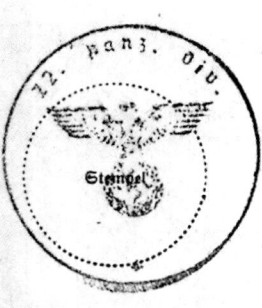

**Possession certificate for the Panzer Assault Badge in Bronze
for an *Oberleutnant* in a rifle regiment.**

Besitzeugnis

Dem   Leutnant
<small>Dienstgrad</small>

     Hannes Truger
<small>Vor- und Familienname</small>

     3./ Panz. Aufkl. Abt. 17
<small>Truppenteil</small>

verleihe ich für tapfere Teilnahme an   25   Einsatztagen

die II. Stufe zum

Panzerkampfabzeichen

in

Bronze

O. U., 1o. Sept. 1944
<small>Ort und Datum</small>

Maier
<small>Unterschrift</small>

Hauptmann u. Abt. Kdr.
<small>Dienstgrad und Dienststellung</small>

(Stamp: Druckstelle Feldpostnummer 23326)

Possession certificate for the Panzer Assault Badge in Bronze, 2nd level, for a *Leutnant* in an armored reconnaissance unit.

An entry in a pass about the award
of the Panzer Assault Badge in Bronze.

The back of a Panzer Assault Badge in Silver
with the manufacturer's initials.

Panzer-Ersatz-Abteilung 7
Abt. IIb

Böblingen, den 27. März 1941.

Ausbildungs-Nachweis

für den am 31.3.1941 zur Panzer-Regt. 201
(Truppenteil)

versetzten Panzerschützen Arthur Großhans
(Dienstgrad) (Name)

1.) Diensteintritt: 3.12.40. bei J.E.B. 35, Pforzheim
Komp. (Einheit)

2.) Ausgebildet als: Panzer-Fahrer

3.) Wehrmachts-Führerschein Kl. I u. II

4.) Sonderausbildung als:

5.) Zur Verwendung als: Panzer-Fahrer

Major und Btl. Kommandeur.

Bem.: Dieser Ausbildungsnachweis wird in je einer Ausfertigung dem Transportführer zur Vorlage bei dem anfordernden Regiment und eine Ausfertigung dem Mann zur Vorlage bei seiner Einheit mitgegeben.

Training certificate for a tank driver.

A n t r a g

auf Verleihung des Panzerkampfabzeichens

in S i l b e r   IV.Stufe

1. Vor- und Familienname	Arthur G r o s s h a n s
2. Dienstgrad	Unteroffizier
3. Truppenteil	2./Pz.Rgt.23
4. Aufführung von mindestens 3 Kampfeinsätzen /Panzerfahrer/	Hat vom 1.4.42 – 30.6.43 einschl. an 23 bestätigten Angriffen, vom 1.7.43 – 9.1.45 einschl. an 52 bestätigten Angriffen teilgenommen.
5. Vermerk über Verleihung und Aushändigung	verl. am 11.1.45 ...

O.U., den 18. Januar 1945

I.V.

[signature]

L e u t n a n t

An entry indicating the award of the Panzer Assault Badge in Silver, 4th level.

34

```
 1. 24. 7.43  Gegenangriff auf Feindpanzer nordostw. Krinitschke
 2. 30. 7.43  Angriff auf Ssaur-Mogilski
 3.  1. 8.43  Angriff auf Krutaja-Schlucht und Marinowka
 4.  5. 8.43  Angriff auf Feindpanzer bei 213,9
 5. 16. 8.43  Angriff auf Höhe 204,0
 6. 17. 8.43  Angriff zur Wiedergewinnung des Geländes bei 185,9 und 204,0
 7. 18. 8.43  Angriff zur Herstellung der alten HKL auf 204,0
 8. 21. 8.43  Angriff auf 204,0
 9. 22. 8.43  Angriff auf 234,6 und Riegelstellung Dolgenkaja
10. 23. 8.43  Angriff auf Feindpanzer bei 242,9
11. 24. 8.43  Angriff auf Feindpanzer bei 229,2
12. 27. 8.43  Kampf gegen Pakfront westl. Dolgenkaja
13.  3. 9.43  Gegenangriffe auf Feindpanzer südwestl. Dolgenkaja
14.  7. 9.43  Angriff auf Nowo-Alexandrowka und Warwarowka
15.  8. 9.43  Angriff auf Marienfeld
16.  9. 9.43  Angriff auf Sslawjanka
17. 10. 9.43  Säuberung des Westteils Sslawjanka
18. 11. 9.43  Angriff auf Wesselyj
19. 31. 7.43  Angriff auf Garany
20. 15. 9.43  Angriff auf Höhe 119,6 und Jekaterinowka
21. 16. 9.43  Angriff auf Höhe 144,6
22. 18. 9.43  Gegenstoss auf Ssoffjewka
23. 20. 9.43  Angriff auf Feindpanzer ostw. Sslawgorod
24. 23. 9.43  Angriff auf Panzergraben bei Ssoffjewka
25.  1.10.43  Angriff auf 70,4 und Vorstoss auf 156,9 zur Entlastung der
            eigenen Infanterie
26.  2.10.43  Abwehr eines russ.Einbruchs bei 122,2 und Wiedereinnahme der
            alten HKL
27.  3.10.43  Kampfe um das Strassenkreuz südl. Mischurin-Rog
28.  4.10.43  Gegenangriff auf 122,2
29.  5.10.43  Gegenangriff auf 106,7 und Strassenkreuz südl.Mischurin-Rog
30. 10. 1.44  Angriff auf Wissokij
31. 11. 1.44  Angriff auf Höhe 138,2
32. 12. 1.44  Angriff auf Höfe Sheltje und Ortrub
33. 16.10.44  Angriff aus Berettyo-Ujfalo nach Norden zur Entlastung von
            Berecske und Zerschlagung von Feindverbänden südwestl.Tep...
34. 18.10.44  Gegenangriff auf Hoszu-Palyi, ostw. Haydu-Bagos
35. 11.11.44  Angriff 3 km südl.Pand im Raume Pz.Gren.Rgt.126 zuer Wieder-
            herstellung der alten HKL
36. 12.11.44  Abwehr eines fdl.Pz.Angriffs südwestl. Jaszbereny
37. 13.11.44  Angriff von Jaszbereny nach Südosten und Südwesten zur Unter-
            stützung der eigenen Infanterie
38. 14.11.44  Abwehr fdl.Inf.Angriff auf den Südteil von Jaszbereny
39. 16.11.44  Abwehr fdl.Inf.-u.Pz.Angriffe nordwestl. Puszta-Monostor
40. 18.11.44  Angriffe auf Höhe 124, 5 km südl. Ujhatvan, zur Wiederherstel-
            lung der alten HKL bei Pz.Gren.Rgt.126
41. 19.11.44  Gegenstoss von Dohany mjr. auf P.117 zur Wiederherstellung der
            alten HKL mit anschl.Abwehr eines fdl.Inf.Angriffs
42. 20.11.44  Angriff auf Gehöft Fekete, ca. 4 km südwestl. Hatvan
43. 21.11.44  Angriff auf fdl.Pz.Bereitstellung östl.Puszta-Nagyhat,
            nordostw.Hatvan
44. 22.11.44  Angriff auf durchgebrochene Feindpanzer und Inf. nördl.P.168,
            4 km nordostw. Hatvan
45. 23.11.44  Angriff im Raum Pz.Gren.Rgt.126 zwischen 135 und 133 gegen
            durchgebrochene fdl. Infanterie
46.  3.12.44  Angriff von Pincehely nach Süden zur Wiederherstellung der HKL
47.  4.12.44  Angriff auf Mezö-Komarom und Höhe 158
48.  5.12.44  Säuberung der Strasse Deg-Lajos-Komarom u.Angriff auf Höhe 176
49.  8.12.44  Angriff auf Polgardi und Wiederinbesitznahme dieses Ortes
50.  9.12.44  Angriff auf Pöttölle und Wiederinbesitznahme dieses Ortes
51. 10.12.44  Angriff auf Bölseberand, 10 km südostw.Stuhlweissenburg und
            Inbesitznahme dieses Ortes
52.  9. 1.45
```

The list of a tank driver's fifty-two confirmed attacks.

Besitzeugnis

Dem **Leutnant**

Stab **†I.** / Panzer=Regiment 11
„v. Hünersdorff"

verleihe ich für tapfere Teilnahme

an **25** Einsatztagen
die **II.** Stufe zum

Panzerkampfabzeichen
Silber

Rgts.=Gef.Stand en 15. 8. 19 4 3

Oberstleutnant u. Rgts.-Kdr.

Westfälisches Volksbu'l, Paderborn

36

Besitzeugnis

Dem   Leutnant

Stab   II. / Panzer-Regiment 11
„v. Hünersdorff'

verleihe ich für tapfere Teilnahme

an   50   Einsatztagen
die   III.   Stufe zum

Panzerkampfabzeichen
Silber

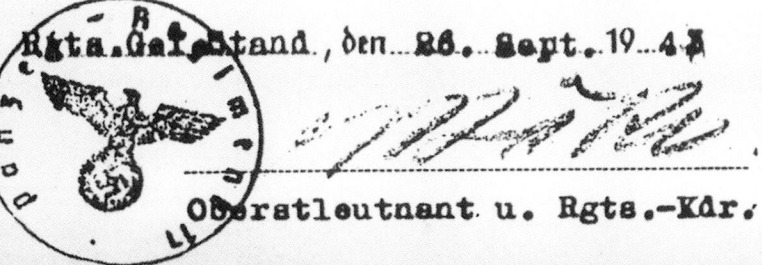

Rgts.-Gef.Stand., den 26. Sept. 19 43

Oberstleutnant. u. Rgts.-Kdr.

Besitzeugnis

Dem   Oberleutnant

Stab   II. / Panzer-Regiment 11
„v. Hünersdorff"

verleihe ich für tapfere Teilnahme

an   75   Einsatztagen
die   IV.   Stufe zum

Panzerkampfabzeichen
Silber

Rgts.Gef.Stand, den 16. März 1944

Oberstleutnant u. Rgts.-Kdr. i.V.

When the enemy artillery began to fire, a dull pressure made itself felt in my stomach. I slid down from my airy seat and exchanged my field cap for a steel helmet. A quick glance around me showed the pale faces of my comrades and the uneasy question of what would happen in the next half-hour. When would the command to attack finally come? In the beginning inferno of the battle there was suddenly roaring and rumbling ahead of us, around us, coming at us. Long flames hissed out of the exhaust pipes of the heavy tanks; rumbling, thundering and rattling, the division rolled ahead…

"Well, finally", I thought, and the *Unterscharführer* called to the driver, "Caracho!" Heavy defensive fire from a Soviet antitank force in a deep location slammed against us. "Make sure that you go there behind the tanks," Behind the steel Colossus we were safe from direct fire. The steel box suddenly stopped, shaking. Thank God we had enough space. "Go around to the left. Press on the tube!" Standing in our SPW, our weapons cocked, we pressed against the tank and another shot-down Panzer IV and passed them – through a minefield directly in front of the antitank force. Past a destroyed enemy gun and fallen Red Army men. Hand grenades exploded, shots came from machine guns, pistols and carbines. Soviets hurrying away sank into flat spots – we were through! After some time the noise faded away. We beckoned to the next wagon and saw the first prisoners. Embarrassed nodding. Only now did we look around us. Our own shot-down tanks, SPW, amphibians – destroyed enemy antitank guns – they burned and smoked everywhere. One man lit a cigarette others reached into an empty ammunition case in which food was packed. But the rest didn't last long; after all, the retreating enemy had to be pursued."

PANZER BADGE

Silver   to members of panzer units

Bronze   to members of rifle, armored grenadier, motorcycle rifle and armored reconnaissance units of the armored divisions.

THE ASSAULT BADGE (GENERAL)

On June 1, 1940 an Assault Badge was introduced that could be awarded to officers, NCOs and men of the service arms that were included neither in the requirements for awarding the Infantry Assault Badge nor those of the Panzer Assault Badge. Required for earning what was first called the Special Assault Badge were participation in:

    – three assault attacks

    – in the foremost line

    – breaking in with weapon in hand

    – on three different combat days.

The silver-colored badge showed a side arm crossed with a stick grenade in a wreath of oak leaves under the symbol of the Wehrmacht. This decoration was originally awarded, like the Panzer Assault Badge, by the tactical superior officer at the rank of division commander. The Assault Badge was awarded to members of the corps, army or Army troops by the division commander to whom the units were subordinated in combat. As of September 9, 1942 the independent battalion and other unit commanders had the right to confer it. The material, production and way of wearing it were like those of the other assault badges. As of June 22, 1943 the Special Assault Badges were called the Assault Badge General (*Allg.*).

Members of the tank destroyer units, artillery regiments and assault gun units fulfilled the requirements when they took part in assaults and had achieved a breakthrough into enemy lines through the use of their weapons in the foremost line. For members of the flak companies who were involved in ground combat, the requirements for the award of the Assault Badge were to be applied in the same way.

ASSAULT BADGE (GENERAL)

To members of artillery, Flak, cavalry, intelligence, tank destroyer, engineer, medical and assault gun units

---

The Higher Levels of the Panzer Assault and Assault (general) Badges

In the Army Information of 1943, under number 575, the regulations as to the introduction of higher levels of the Panzer Assault Badge and Assault Badge (general) as of June 22, 1943 were published:

"1. The *Führer* has authorized the introduction of higher levels of the Panzer Assault Badge in recognition of the repeatedly shown joy of action of the tank-attacking members of the heavy weapons.

2. The higher levels of the Panzer Assault Badge will be made to a particular pattern with the number 25 for the second, the number 50 for the third, and the numbers 75 and 100 for the fourth level.

3. It can be awarded:

   After 25 recorded actions, the second level,

   After 50 recorded actions, the third level,

   After 75 recorded actions, the fourth level,

   And, in fact,

   The Panzer Assault Badge in Silver, to tank crews of the tank units, Panzer Assault Badge in Bronze to tank crews of the armored reconnaissance units, the Assault Badge (general) to members of assault units, the assault armored and tank destroyer units of the tank destroyer forces (Sf.)

   The fourth level can be awarded again after 100 actions with the number 100.

4. Only one Assault Badge may be worn, but the lower levels remain for remembrance.

5. The eligibility of the combat days for inclusion results from the requirements for the awarding of the Panzer Assault Badge and the Assault Badge (general), for the assault gun units and the tank destroyer units of the tank destroyer forces (Sf.), the requirements stated for the members of the assault gun batteries apply here.

6. The company or other leader provides a list of the names of the soldiers who took part in and proved themselves in an eligible combat day, to be concluded after the last entry with the signature of the unit leader and service stamp. These lists are to be in the additions to the war diary.

7. Every man is to carry in his *soldbuch* a sheet on which the eligible combat day is to be noted and documented.

8. a) The combat days for the higher levels of the Panzer Assault Badge and Assault Badge (general) are to be counted as of 7/1/1943; for the already awarded Infantry Assault Badge, Panzer Assault Badge or Assault Badge (general), though, three combat days from the period before 7/1/1943 are reckoned without further documentation.

   b) Beyond that, in order to elevate the proved veteran front fighter, for unbroken combat in the East or in Africa after 6/22/1941, there can

   from 15 months, up to 25 combat days

   from 12 months, up to 15 combat days

   from 8 months, up to 10 combat days

   be counted through evidence gained by conscientious checking of the combat leader. Command, wounding, freezing or furlough up to one quarter of the foreseen periods do not count as interruption of the combat.

   The combat days are to be determined by the regimental or other commander for the units on request from the company or other leader.

A bearer of the Assault Badge (general)

The Assault Badge (general)

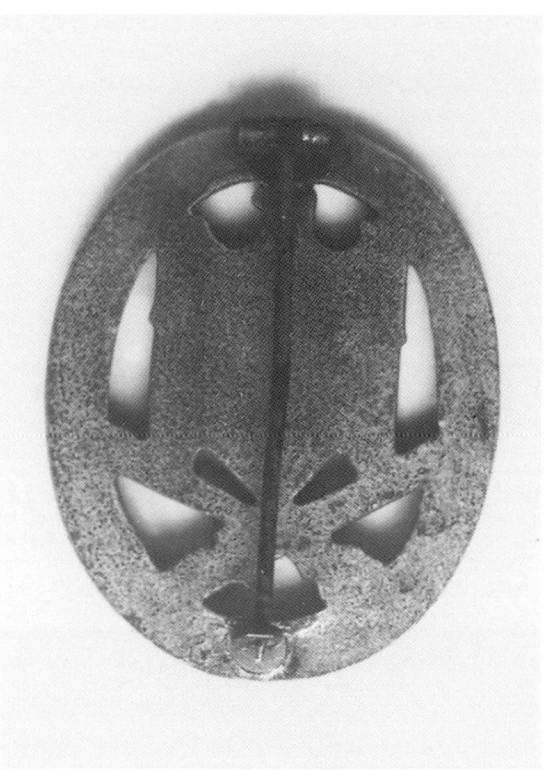

The backs of the various assault badges (general) with different pin systems

Assault Badge 2nd level for 25 combat days   **Assault Badge 3rd level for 50 combat days**

Back of the 2nd and 3rd level badges

Assault Badge 4th level for 75 combat days

Assault Badge 4th level for 100 days

Back of the two 4th level badges

Erich Thoele, as a member of the SS Cavalry Division,
received the Assault Badge (general).

Besitzeugnis

Dem .... Obergefreiten ....
(Dienstgrad)

.... Hans O v e r ....
(Vor- und Zuname)

3. / Sturmgeschütz - Abteilung 249
(Truppenteil)

wurde das

Sturmabzeichen

verliehen.

Abt.Gef.St., 5.11.1943.
(Ort und Datum)

(Unterschrift)

Hauptmann und Abteilungs-
kommandeur
(Dienstgrad und Dienststellung)

Stempel

**Possession certificate for the Assault Badge (general)
for an *Obergefreiter* in an assault gun unit.**

BESITZZEUGNIS

DEM   Obergefreiten
(DIENSTGRAD)

Hans Over
(VOR- UND FAMILIENNAME)

3. / Heeres - Sturmgeschütz - Brigade 249
(TRUPPENTEIL)

VERLEIHE ICH FÜR TAPFERE TEILNAHME
AN 25 EINSATZTAGEN

DIE II. STUFE ZUM
STURMABZEICHEN

Im Feld, den 16. 11. 1944
(ORT UND DATUM)

(UNTERSCHRIFT)

Hauptmann und Kommandeur
Heeres-Sturmgeschütz-Brigade
(DIENSTGRAD UND DIENSTSTELLUNG)

(STEMPEL)

Possession certificate for the 2nd level of the Assault Badge (general)
for an *Obergefreiter* in an Army assault gun brigade.

49

Besitzeugnis

Dem   Obergefreiten

(Dienstgrad)

Paul Grundmann

(Vor- und Zuname)

A. A. 23

(Truppenteil)

verleihe ich das

Infanterie-Sturmabzeichen

— Silber —

Im Felde, den 4.5.1942.

(Ort und Datum)

J. V.

[signature]

(Unterschrift)

Hauptmann und stellv.
Rgts.-Führer.

(Dienstgrad und Dienststellung)

Stempel

Non-permitted awarding of two Assault Badges to the same soldier.

Besitzeugnis

Dem   Obergefreiten
(Dienstgrad)

Paul Grundmann
(Vor- und Zuname)

4./Radfahr-Bataillon 23
(Truppenteil)

wurde das

Sturmabzeichen

verliehen.

Div.St.Qu., den 20.8.1942
(Ort und Datum)

Mit der Führung beauftragt

(Unterschrift)

Oberst
(Dienstgrad und Dienststellung)

c) The division commander can award the higher levels of the Panzer Assault Badge (general) to soldiers for whom, because of serious wounding, no opportunity for recordable action in the future is possible. The recipient must show for the award of

the second level, at least 18 combat days

the third level, at least 35 combat days

the fourth level, at least 60 combat days.

For the reckoning of combat days before 7/1/1943, see above under b).

9. Recipients are to have possession certificates filled out by the awarding regimental or other commanders.

10. The requirements for the awarding of the Panzer Assault Badge and Assault Badge (general) are the same as those for the awarding of the higher levels, as long as no special regulation is stated above.

11. The monthly need for higher levels of the Panzer Assault Badge and Assault Badge is to be requested by OKH/PA/P5 (f) as gathered from the army groups and independent APKs for all subordinated units as of the 15th of each month.

Deputized for Schmundt
OKH 7/2/1943 13053/43/-P5 (f)."

On September 4, 1944 the Army High Command extended the groups of persons to whom the higher levels of the Assault Badge (general) could be awarded. Thus the badges could be awarded not only to members of:

– the assault gun units,

– the assault tank units,

– the tank destroyer units of the tank destroyer forces (Sf.)

But also, from now on, to members of:

– the armored artillery,

As long as the combat was carried out as escort artillery on tank attacks.

The Panzer Assault Badges of the second and third levels resembled those of the first level (three combat days) and were generally made of fine zinc. But under the tank, which was attached to the oak-leaf wreath with two rivets, were the small plates for 25 or 50 combat days. The two fourth levels had a heavier, gilded oak-leaf wreath on which either a silver or bronze tank was riveted. Under it was the small plate for 75 or 100 combat days.

The Assault Badge (general) was also made of fine zinc as a rule, and showed under the eagle attached with two rivets the number 25 or 50. For the two fourth levels the eagle was riveted to a heavier, gilded oak-leaf wreath. Under it was the small plate for 75 or 100 combat days.

ASSAULT BADGE FOR MEDICAL CORPSMEN

The requirement *"breaking in with weapon in hand"* was regarded as fulfilled for medical officers and medical personnel when they, under the same combat requirements as the assaulting infantry, treated and rescued wounded men in the close combat area.

The medics received the Assault Badge of the applicable troop unit to which they belonged in action, such as:

- an infantry or mountain rifle regiment, the Infantry Assault Badge in Silver

- an infantry regiment (mot.), the Infantry Assault Badge in Bronze

- an artillery regiment, the Assault Badge (general)

- an armored grenadier regiment of an armored division, the Panzer Assault Badge in Bronze

- an armored regiment, the Panzer Assault Badge in Silver.

If the soldiers saw action within a medical unit, they nevertheless received the Assault Badge (general).

BIBLIOGRAPHY

Army Regulation Sheets
1939, Part B, of 12/27/1939, pp.389 ff.
1940, Part B, No.536, 537
1941, Part C, No.211, 449 I, 907
1942, Part B, No.261 I, II, III, 449 II, 647, 687
1942, Part C, No.760
1943, Part C, No.699

General Army Announcements
1942, No.882
1943, No.12, 65, 575
1944, No.513, 514

Notice Sheet 15/5, as of 5/1/1943
OKH, P5 (f)/Az 29e general/No.13035/43, June 4, 1943

Michaelis, Rolf, "Zur Verleihungspraxis der Sturmabzeichen des Heeres", in
    INFO Magazin, No.55, Garbsen, 1988.

Michaelis, Rolf, "Das Infanterie-Sturmabzeichen" in Militaria, Norderstedt,
    1989.

Michaelis, Rolf, *Die Sturmabzeichen des Heeres*, Erlangen, 1996.

Other Books by Rolf Michaelis

SS-Heimwehr Danzig in Poland 1939

SS-Fallschirmjäger-Bataillon 500/600

The 10th SS-Panzer-Division "Frundsberg"

The 11th SS-Freiwilligen-Panzer-Grenadier-Division "Nordland"

The 32nd SS-Freiwilligen-Grenadier-Division: "30.Januar"

Combat Operations of the German Ordnungspolizei,
1939-1945: Polizei-Bataillone • SS-Polizei-Regimenter

Cavalry Divisions of the Waffen-SS

Panzergrenadier Divisions of the Waffen-SS

The Kaminski Brigade

Belgians in the Waffen-SS

The German Sniper Badge 1944-1945

The German Tank Destruction Badge in World War II

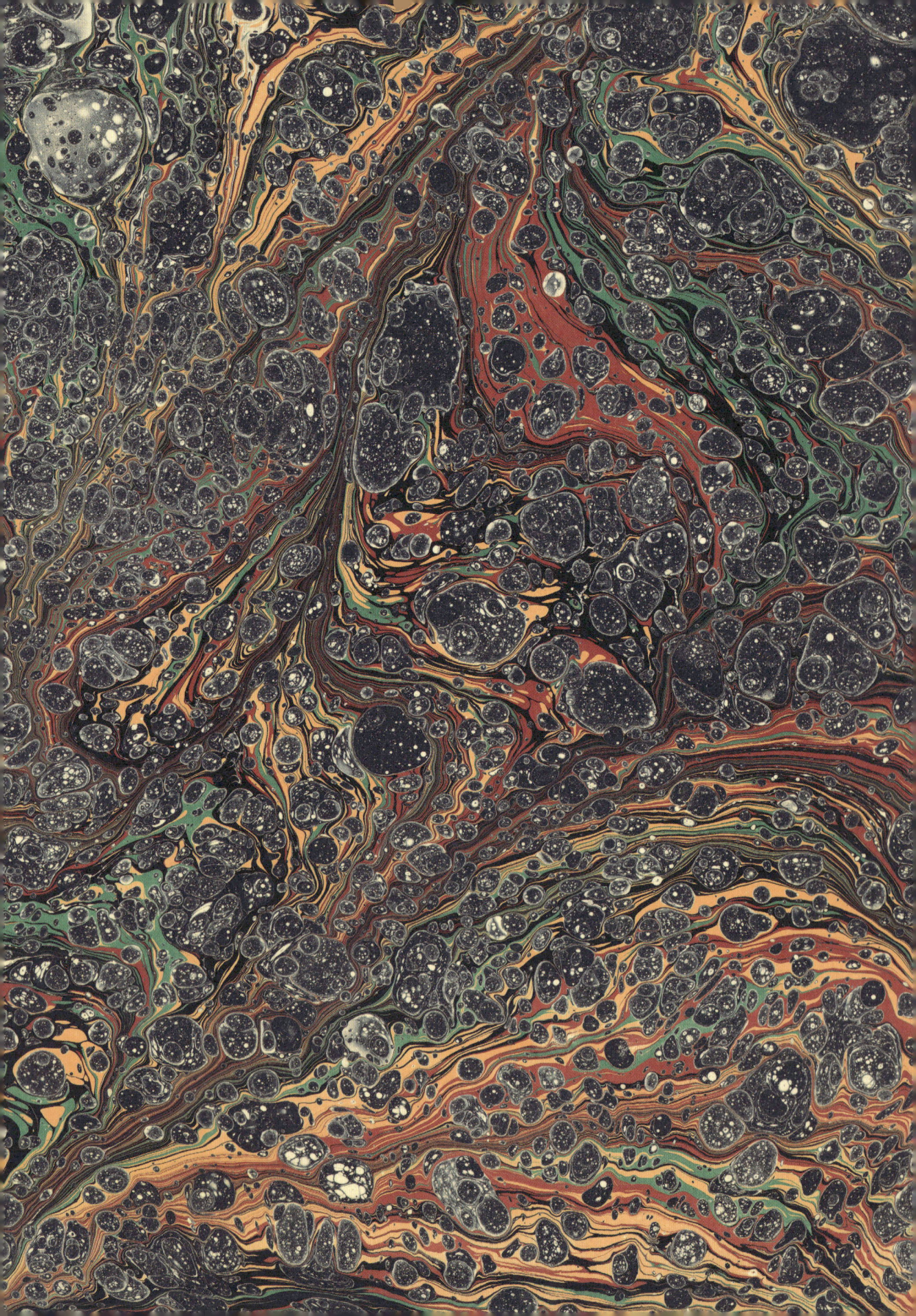